STAINED GLASS
BEVEL WINDOW DESIGNS

Wardell residence

By Randy and Judy Wardell

Published and

Printed in Canada

by

Wardell
PUBLICATIONS

RR 5 Belleville, Ontario Canada K8N 4Z5

D1211773

Lietaer residence

Lietaer residence

Lietaer residence

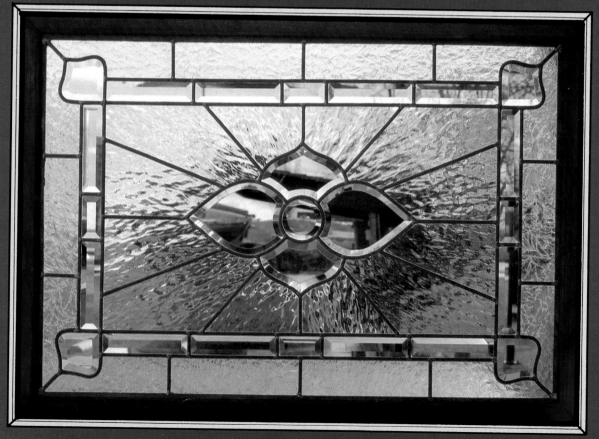

Limestone Café

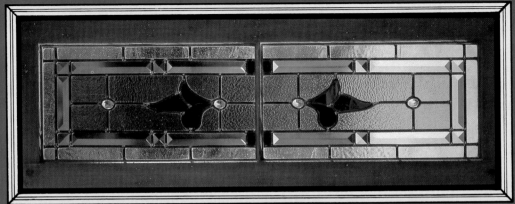

Bradden residence

Wardell residence

Bradden residence

Gregory residence

McCutcheon residence

Sandpiper Studios

McCutcheon residence

McCutcheon residence

Wardell residence

Sandpiper Studios

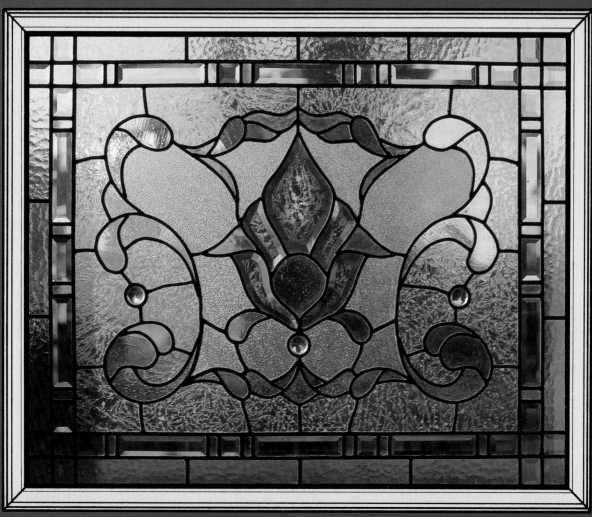

Lietaer residence

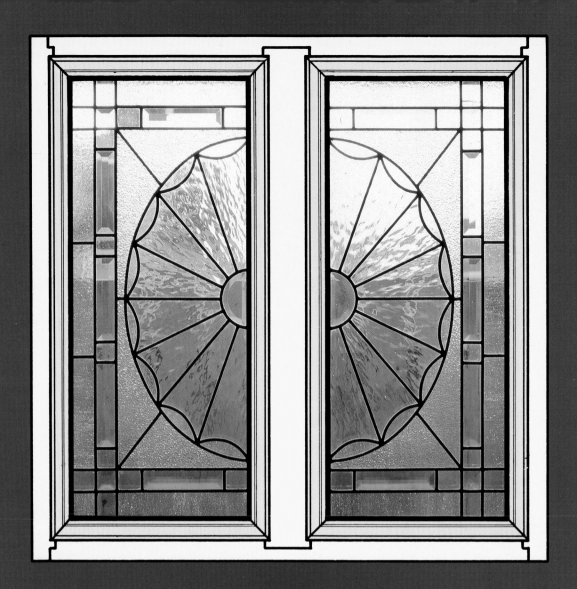

McCutcheon residence

STAINED GLASS
BEVEL WINDOW DESIGNS

by Randy and Judy Wardell

Typesetting and Layout
Steve Campbell, Janet Moore
County Magazine Printshop Ltd.

Photography
Randy and Judy Wardell

Printed in Canada
by
Thorn Press

Special Thanks
Bill Dick
Linda Holmes
Rob Huffman
Mary Hurtzig

Wardell
P U B L I C A T I O N S

RR 5 Belleville, Ontario, Canada K8N 4Z5

PREFACE

We live in a city that has many fine old Victorian homes. Most have made extensive use of beveled glass, especially in the main entry doors and windows. As you walk past these homes at night your eye is treated to a sparkling show as the light from inside is bent and twisted by the beveled glass edges. The daytime experience is even more exciting. As the sunlight passes through the clear beveled window it is magically transformed into hundreds of brightly colored rainbows projected onto the walls and floor. Movement and mystery from a leaded glass window.

In recent years designers have been incorporating beveled glass windows into more and more public buildings and private dwellings. Glass studios are enjoying an increase in beveled window commissions and many new glass beveling companies have been created to meet the demand for special shapes and sizes.

The purpose of this book is to explore the design possibilities using beveled and faceted glass. We wanted to include design styles which use bevels in the border and center in the traditional manner, as well as some with a more modern approach using shaped bevels in the border only. Many of the designs we came up with required custom beveling which could make them cost prohibitive to many hobbiests and small studios. Wardell Publications decided to work with Bevel King™, a bevel manufacturer, to produce our new bevel designs as common stock shapes. These new shapes include corner clusters, center crests and shaped border clusters.

We have included something new we know you will find helpful. Along with the completed design you will notice 'frame blanks' in various sizes and shapes. These blanks can be photocopied and used as a starting point for your own custom designs for yourself or as a presentation to your client.

We hope this book will prove useful when you are researching for a commission or for your own pleasure. Bevels and jewels will add sparkle to your windows just as they did for the craftsmen of the Victorian age.

Canadian Cataloguing in Publication Data

Wardell, Randy A. (Randy Allan), 1954-
Stained glass bevel window designs
ISBN 0-919985-07-6
1. Glass painting and staining - Patterns.
2. Windows. I. Wardell, Judy, 1956-
II. Title.
TT298.W37 1986 748.8 C86-094917-6

CONTENTS

**NOTE: Scale of drawings 1/5th or 20% of full size.
To increase these drawings to full size, multiply the
dimensions by 5 (or scale up to 500%).**

Some of the designs contained in this collection are available as full-size pattern drawings. The majority, however, are small drawings which you will have to scale up to the full-size version. (Scale of drawings 1/5th or 20% of full size. To increase these drawings to full size, multiply the dimensions by 5 or scale up to 500%.) There are several ways to do this and the style of the design will influence the method of use.

As the title suggests, this book deals primarily with bevel window designs. These windows usually consist of a bevel border and possibly one or two additional borders. The design contained inside these borders could be a bevel cluster and goemetric background or a non-geometric design such as a floral pattern or landscape scene. In either case, when working with bevel borders the first few steps are exactly the same.

LAYOUTS AND BORDERS:

Step 1. Layout the full-size dimensions of the window as required. Start by drawing a cross in the center of your paper (using a square). Next divide the width dimension in half and place this 'half-way' mark on the center layout line and towards one end. Mark off the two outside edge dimensions of the window. Move the ruler to the other end of the center layout line and again mark the two outside edges. Repeat this procedure for the length dimension. Finally join these marks to form an accurate and 'squared' layout for your window.

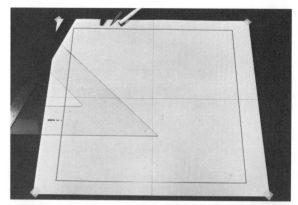

Step 2. If you have already purchased the border bevels for this project, the easiest way to determine the location of the border is to actually place the bevels on the drawing layout where they should go. Carefully line them up (if you are going to use lead came leave the appropriate space between each one) and stand back to see how they look.

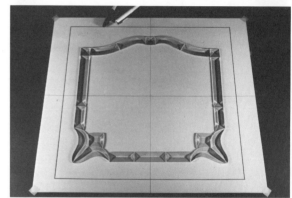

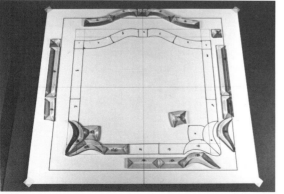

Step 3. When you are satisfied with the bevel border layout, carefully measure the length and width of the bevel borders (which will include the spaces) and write them down. Remove the bevels from the drawing. Mark and draw the bevel border dimensions in the same manner as the outside edges in Step 1. Mark and draw the parallel line for the other edge of the bevel pieces (1" bevel, 1½" bevel, etc.) **NOTE:** Don't assume that the bevels you bought are exactly the width as stated, measure a few just to be on the safe side.

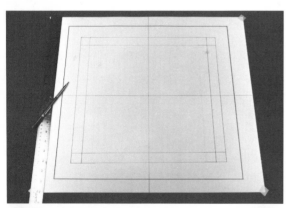

Step 4. Place the bevels back on the drawing and mark the dividing lines by tracing the edge of the bevels. If you are using one of the irregular border clusters or a corner cluster, trace each bevel in its place. Number each bevel and its location on the drawing as you go (all bevels are not created equal), remove and wrap them in newspaper to protect them from scratches until they are needed. If additional borders are required, mark and draw them in at this time.

Once you have completed the border section of the drawing, you must turn your attention to the internal design. The method you use to accomplish this will depend on the design. Read through each method to decide which is best for your window style.

Method A— Trace and measure:

This method is primarily for designs containing a central bevel cluster (or clusters) with a geometric patterned background.

1. If you are using a central bevel cluster, place it on the border drawing and line it up with the layout lines. Trace each bevel in the cluster and number them and their location on the drawing. Remove the cluster and set aside.

2. Divide the background into the desired pattern which could be squares, rectangles, diamonds, symmetrical lines, etc. If the design calls for other accent pieces such as jewels or bevels, place them in the appropriate location and trace them onto the drawing (number each one).

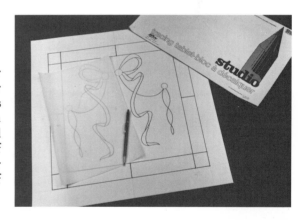

3. Occasionally a design contains a non-bevel shape on one side of center and the reversed image is on the other side. You can reverse and transfer this image easily using a type of paper called 'tracing paper' (also known as onion skin or drafting vellum). It is a semi see-through paper that you simply place over the shape you need to reverse, trace with a soft lead pencil (HB), turn the paper over (face side down) position it on the other side of center and retrace the pencil lines. When you remove the tracing paper enough of the lead pencil will have been rubbed off to leave a clear image of the shape on your drawing, in reverse.

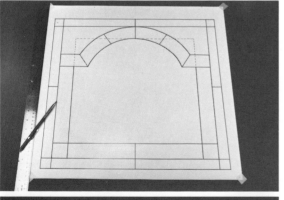

4. Diamond backgrounds: To properly divide a background into equal diamond shapes, you must start with a square or a rectangle of the background area. If, for example, your window contains an irregular border cluster, you must square the cluster ends and extend the side border lines to meet this new line. (See dash lines in photograph.)

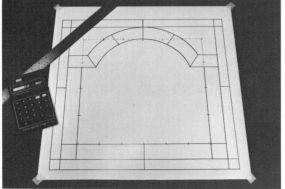

5. Next measure the height and divide it into the desired number of sections (try to make at least four sections). Measure and mark this dimension on both sides. Do the same for the width but make sure the sections are at least 1/3 smaller than those on the height (e.g. if the first sections were 7" long, the short side sections should be 4" to 5").

6. Finally, join the marks. Start at one corner and join the first two marks out from that corner, then join the second two marks and so on until you reach the corner diagonally across. Repeat these steps for the other direction. You should have perfectly shaped diamonds with corners that start and stop at the background edges. **Note:** Don't forget to count the corners as one of the marks.

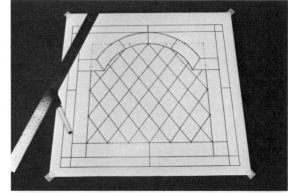

Method B— Grid System:

This is the best system to use when enlarging a random style design such as a floral pattern, a landscape, an animal, etc. It is relatively quick and easy to do even for those of you who say you can't draw a straight line.

1. With your small drawing, measure the design area to be enlarged (that is the inside design, not the borders). Divide this dimension into equal parts as close to 1" as possible (eg. divide 12½" into 12 parts). Do the same with the other dimension. Mark these divisions on your small drawing and divide it into squares.

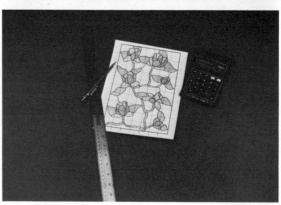

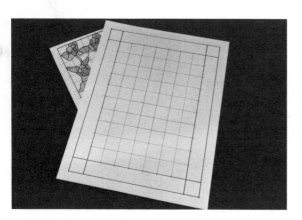

2. Prepare the border as described in the section Layouts and Borders. Measure the design area on this full-size drawing that compares to the area you divided in Step 1 above. Divide this dimension into the same number of sections as in the small drawing (eg. if the size were, say, 36" divide it into 12 parts = 3"). Do the same with the other dimension. Mark these divisions on your full-size drawing and divide it into squares. **Note:** Use a light pencil line that will be easy to erase.

3. Now, simply fill one square at a time on the full-size drawing with the lines as you see them on the small drawing. Work your way across and down until all squares are complete. You can then stand back and have a look. Clean up any lines you feel are not quite correct. Finally, erase the grid lines.

Method C— Mechanical Enlargement:

There are several ways to enlarge a small drawing using machines designed for just such a purpose. Most printing firms have a photographic machine called a process camera which can enlarge a small drawing to exact dimensions. Many photocopiers have enlarging capabilities, however a serious drawback is the limitation in size (usually a maximum size of 11"x 17"). Very small drawings (3"x 3") can be enlarged using an opaque projector. Your drawing goes under the projector and the image is enlarged onto a wall where it can be traced onto your paper. If speed is not important, you could take a slide photograph of your drawing with a 35 mm camera and project it onto your paper to trace. Ask your glass retailer for information on the availability of these services in your area.

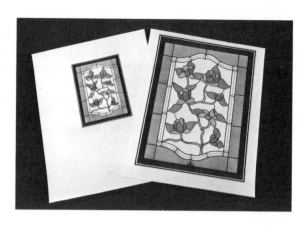

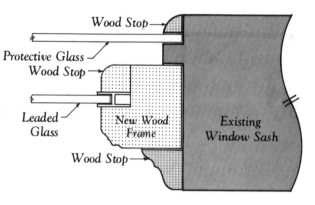

Direct installation with a wood frame

INSTALLING AND REINFORCING YOUR WINDOW

A stained glass window is not fully complete until it has been placed in a location for viewing. Often a window is conceived and constructed for a specific spot and must be sized to fit accordingly. This could include a permanent type of installation such as in a door or directly into a window sash. It could be a semi-permanent installation such as a custom window and frame sized to free-hang in front of an existing window. An increasingly popular style of installation is the autonomous (independent) panel. This type of window, although not constructed for a particular location, nevertheless must be framed and ready to hang (eventually) in a window.

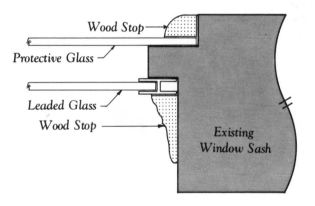

Direct installation without a wood frame

FRAMING/INSTALLATION METHODS:

1. Direct Installation: The most common way to permanently install a panel is to fit it directly into the window sash or door frame. Often you will find a wood stop already attached to the window sash (if one is not already there, a 3/8"x 3/8" square stop can easily be nailed to the sash). The existing clear glass can be left in place to act as protection for the new panel. Place your window against the wood stop and finish with a fancy wood stop (¼" quarter round) or glazier points and putty. If there is not enough room in the sash for this type of installation you may have to replace the existing clear glass with your new panel.

2. Wood Frame Installation: There is a great variety of manufactured wood frames in many stock sizes and shapes. Most glass retailers will have a selection of these frames and many will order (or make) a custom sized frame for you. Purchase the frame and take accurate measurements before you begin drawing or construction of your window. If you intend to order a custom sized frame which must fit into an opening in a wall or door, tell the framer your dimensions are for 'overall' frame size (the window or 'glass size' will be smaller). You would be wise to delay construction of the panel until you have received the frame.

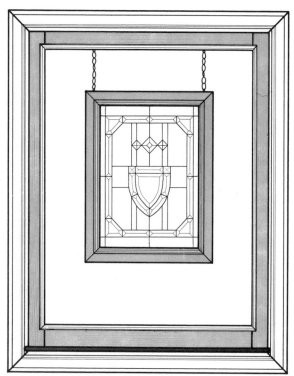

Free hanging autonomous panel

3. Autonomous panel: This independant window is not usually designed for a specific location but rather to be framed and hung in front of any window or light source. It could be framed in wood as described above or framed using zinc, brass, copper, or lead came. Regardless of the frame used the panel will require at least two loops at the top where chain or cord can be attached to allow it to be hung. If a wood frame is used, screw eyes can be inserted, one in each top corner. The metal frame will require a loop formed using at least a 12 gauge wire and soldered to the outer edge of the top corners.

4. Reinforcing Your Window: A large panel, once installed, will bow or sag under its own weight if not reinforced with steel bars. This is particularly true of windows containing bevels due to the extra weight the bevels add. A general 'rule of thumb' is any window 6 square feet or larger (4 square feet if it contains bevels), especially if it is to be installed in a door, should be reinforced.

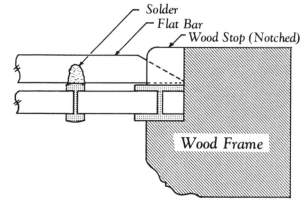

The traditional method is to fasten round steel bars to the window by tying them with copper wire that has been soldered to the leads. A more recent method is to use a flat steel bar (1/8"x 1/2") which can be bent to follow a lead or soldered foil seam from one edge to the other. The bar is usually made from steel, galvanized (coated) with tin so that it can be soldered directly to the seam it is following. The ends of the bar are then attached to the window frame during installation.

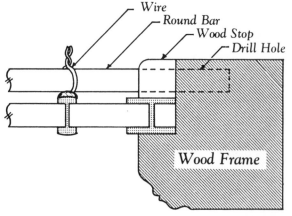

CUT AND PASTE BEVEL DESIGNING

When you sit down to design a window, often the most difficult task is deciding on a place to start. We have devised a method you can use to make choices and changes in a design quickly and easily to help you or your client visualize the window.

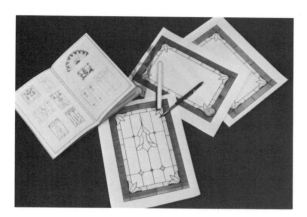

As you look through the drawings in this book you will notice 'blank' frames in each section along with the fully designed windows. These blanks can be used by you to fill with your own design ideas. It is best to make some photocopies of the blank you want to use and sketch your design ideas on these. This will allow you to make several versions of your window design to compare before making the final choice.

The dimension listed with each blank is the size the full-size window would be if it were constructed using the bevels and border as shown. However, size adjustments can be made quite easily by reducing or enlarging the outer border or by adding an additional border. More often than not, one dimension will have to be expanded more than the other. This is not such a problem provided the top border matches the bottom and the right side matches the left.

The last few pages of the book contain scale drawings of the bevel clusters we used in the window drawings. As well, there is a list of common sizes for straight and shaped bevels stocked by most glass supply shops. These clusters are drawn to the same scale as the blank frames to allow you to design your own custom bevel window. Make a photocopy of the cluster pages. Choose a cluster, cut it out of the paper and position it on a copy of the blank frame you want to use. If it suits your design needs, paste it down.

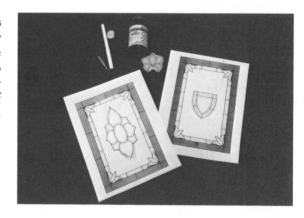

Complete the design with additional bevel shapes or a pattern of your own. Finally, break up the background with a geometric pattern such as squares, diamonds or other style. To get a really good idea of how the completed window will look, use pencil crayons or water paints to color your 'cartoon sketch'.

16"x 36"

16"x 36"

16"x 36"

16"x 36"

16"x 22"

16"x 22"

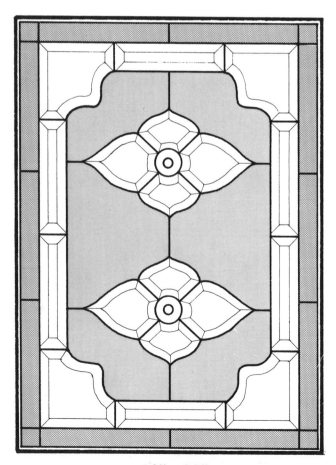

16"x 22"

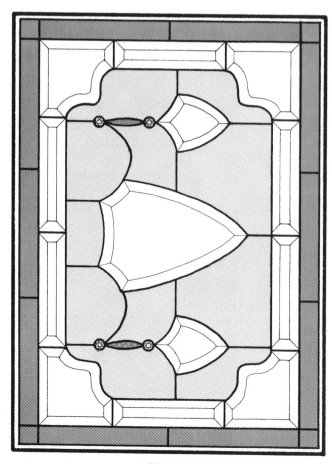

16"x 22"

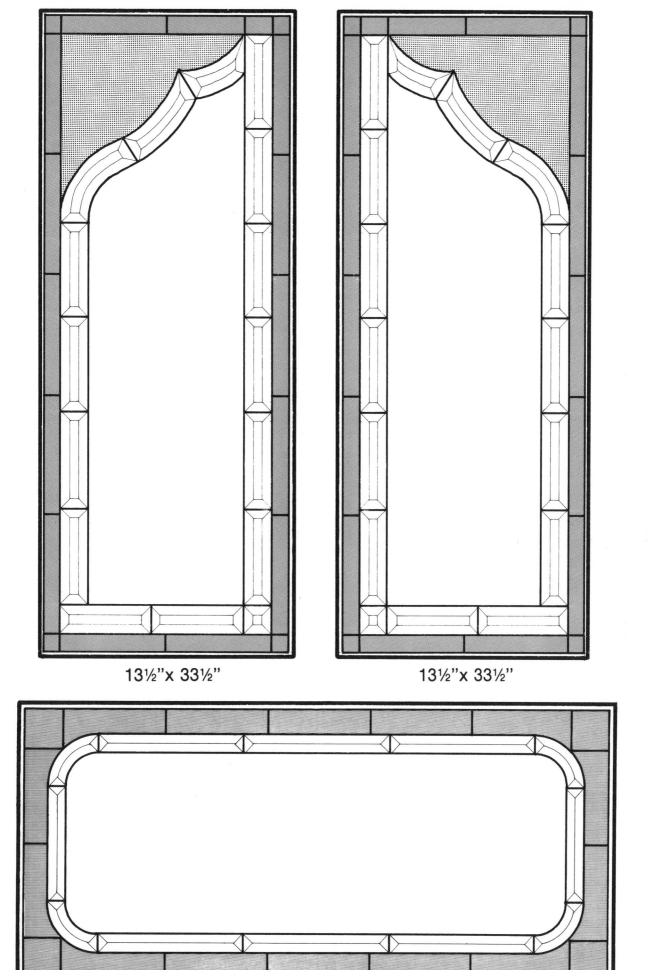

13½"x 33½"   13½"x 33½"

32"x 14"

13½"x 33½"   13½"x 33½"

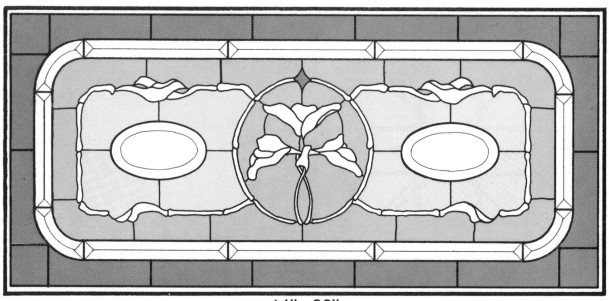

14"x 32"

13½"x 33½"   13½"x 33½"

14"x 32"

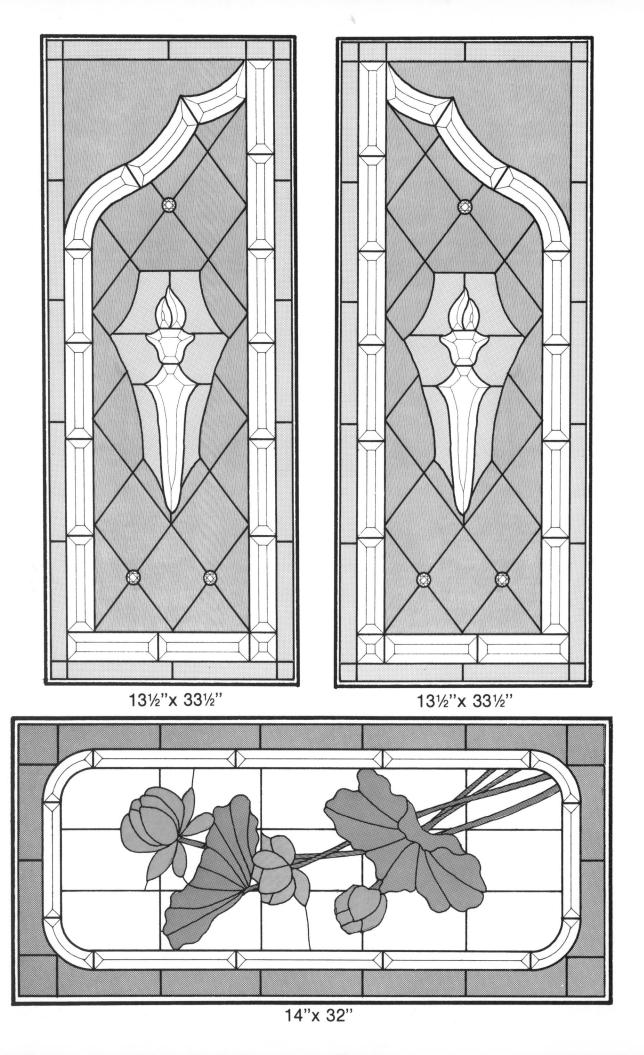

13½"x 33½"   13½"x 33½"

14"x 32"

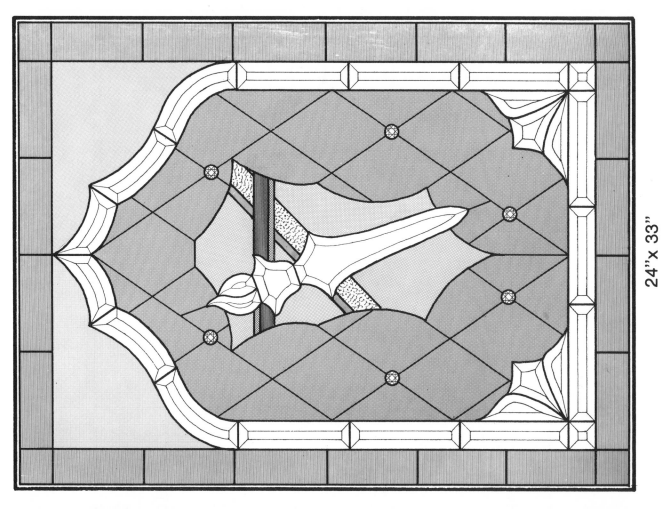

24"x 33"

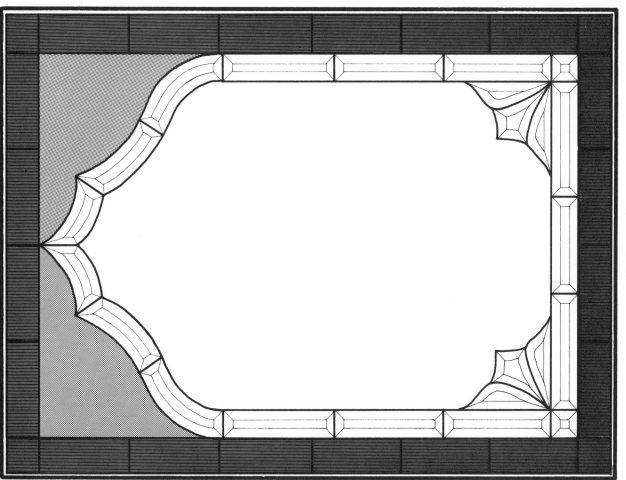

24"x 33"

25

24"x 33"

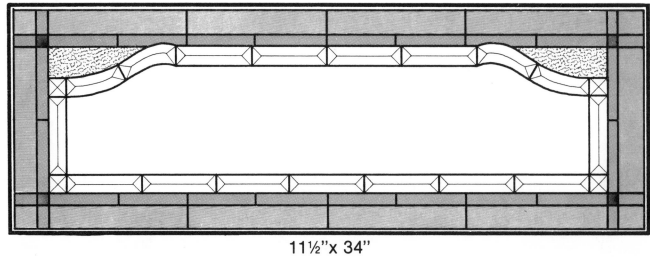

11½"x 34"

21"x 31½"

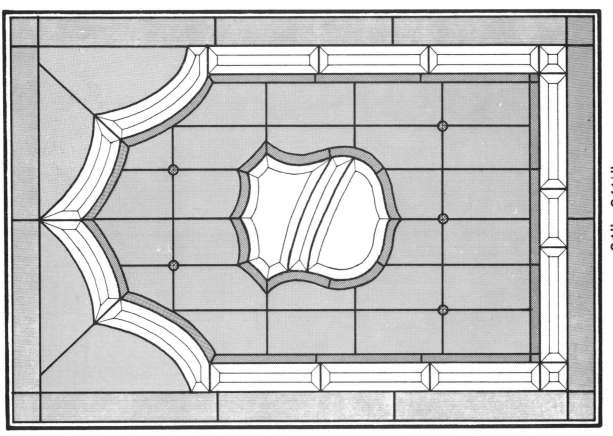

21"x 31½"

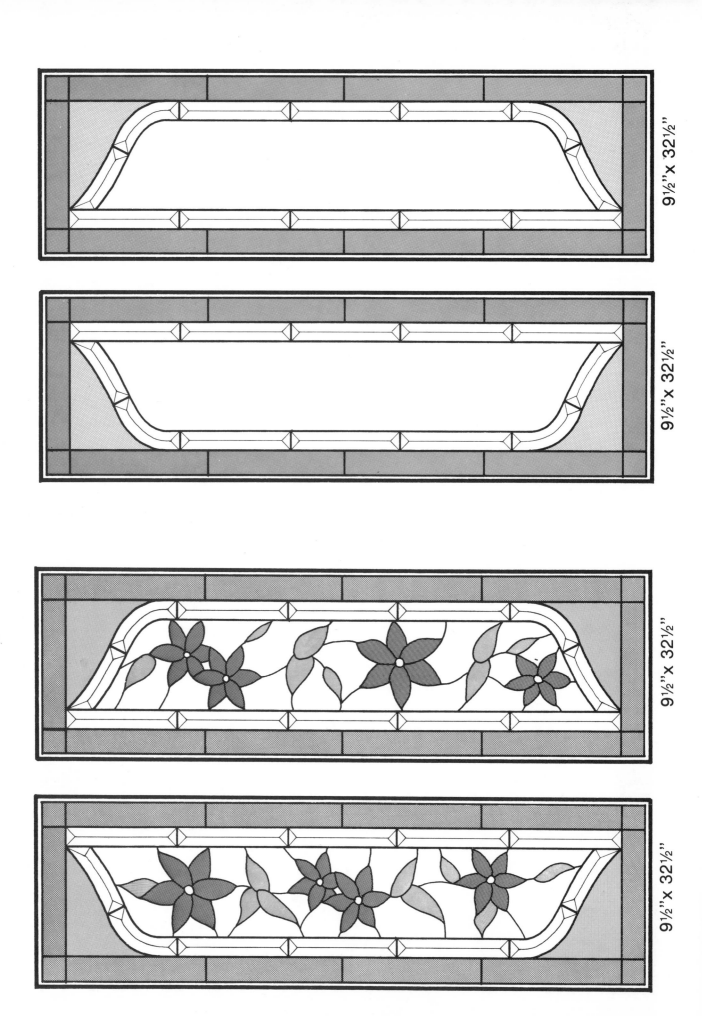

9½" x 32½"

9½" x 32½"

9½" x 32½"

9½" x 32½"

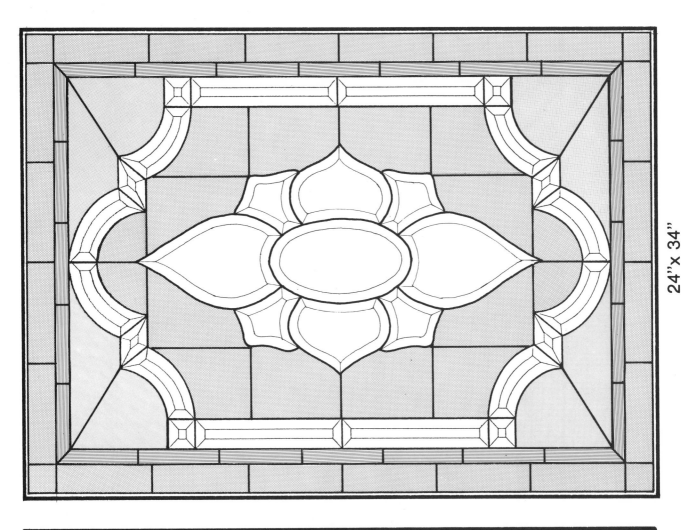

24"x 34"

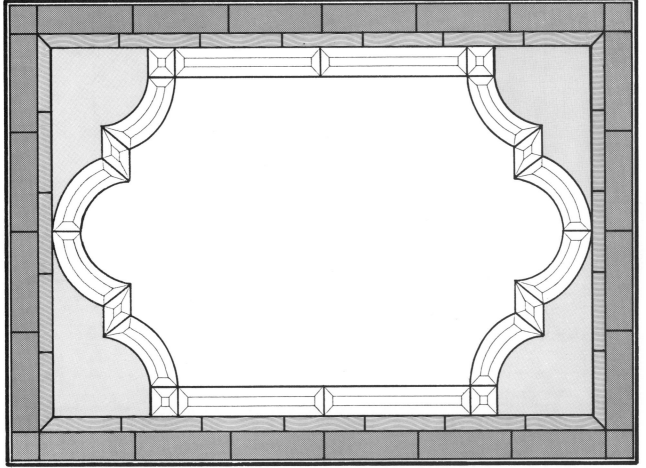

24"x 34"

24"x 34"

11½"x 34"

24"x 34"

21"x 21"

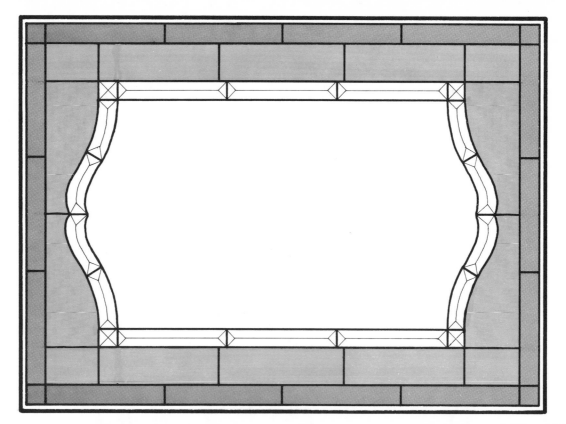

20"x 28"

20"x 28"

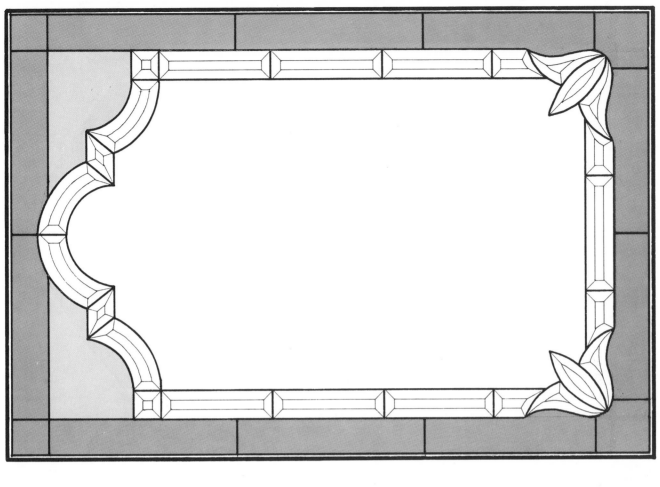

23"x 35"

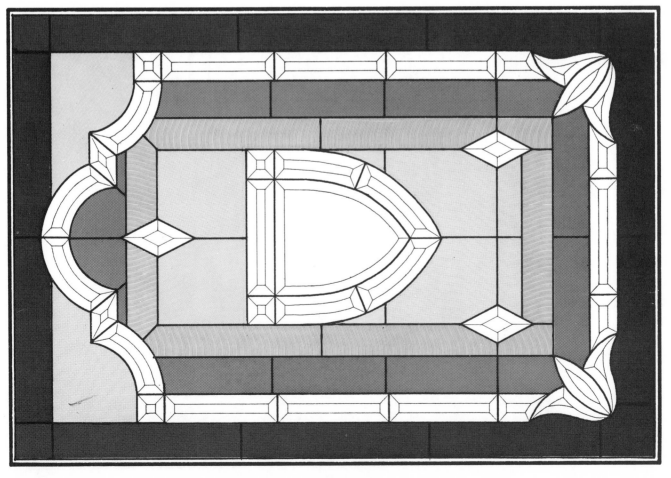

23"x 35"

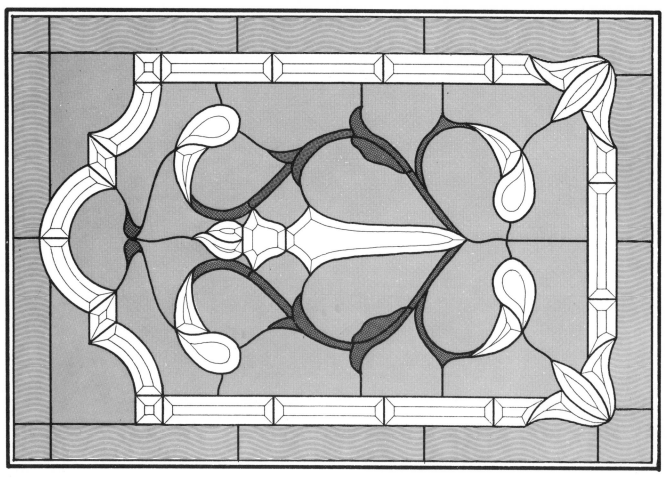

23"x 35"

23"x 35"

34

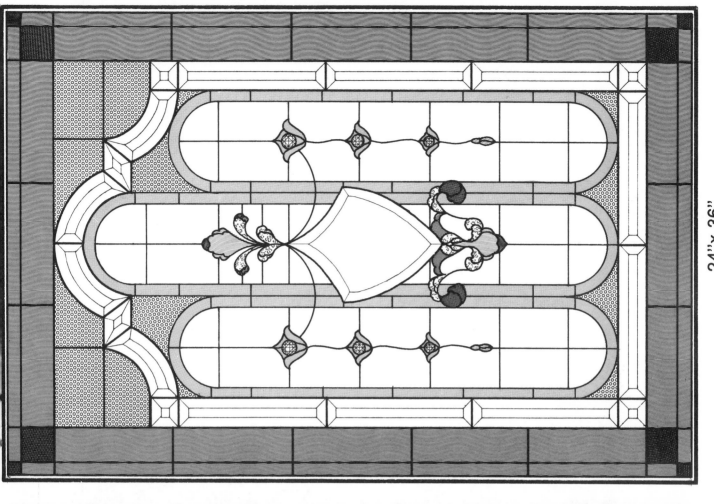

24"x 36"

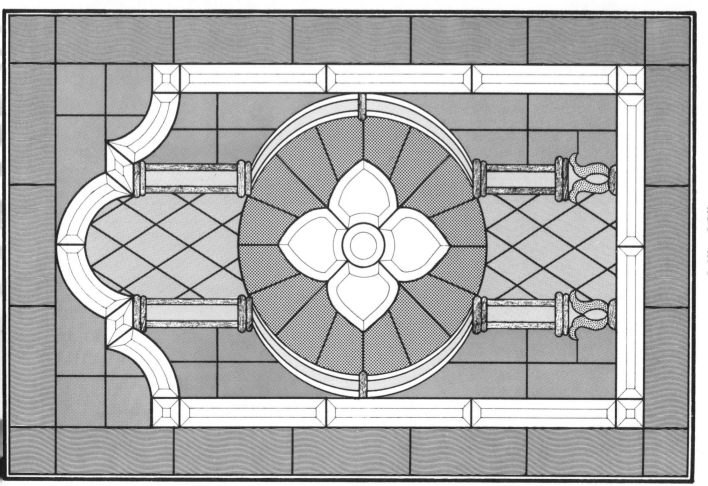

24"x 36"

35

30"x 30"

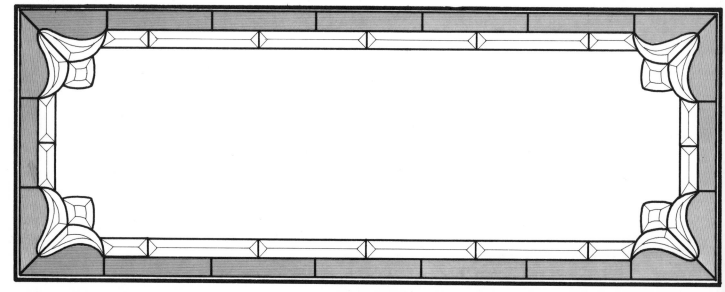

14"x 38"

30"x 30"

14"x 38"

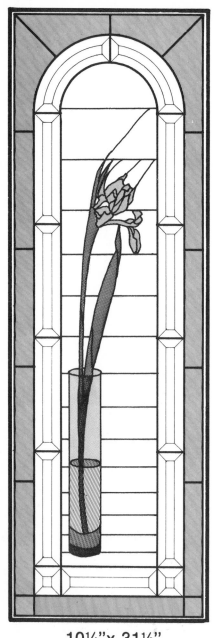

10¼"x 31½"

10¼"x 31½"

10¼"x 31½"

16¼"x 32¾"

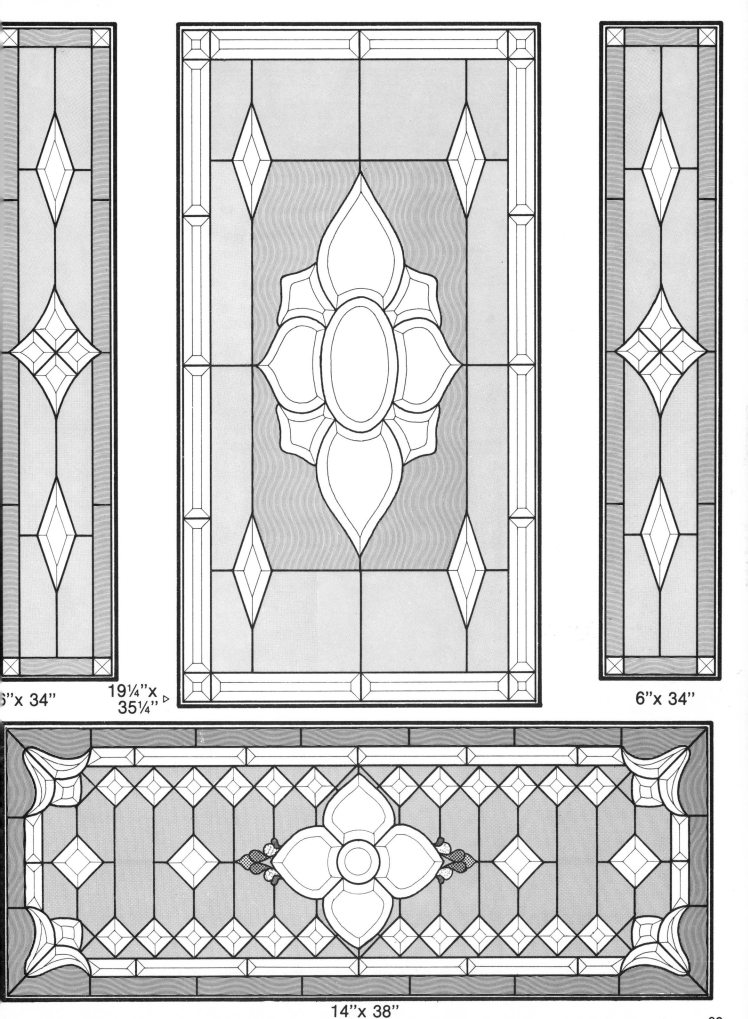

6"x 34"

19¼"x ▷
35¼"

6"x 34"

14"x 38"

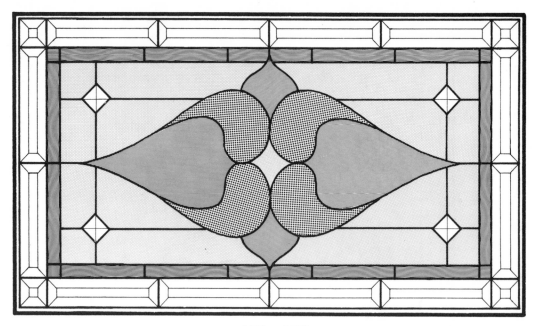

15"x 27"

15"x 27"

20"x 25½"

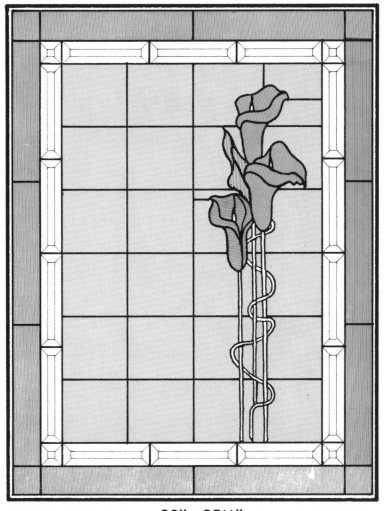

20"x 25½"

13½"x 31"

13½"x 31"

13"x 17"

13"x 17"

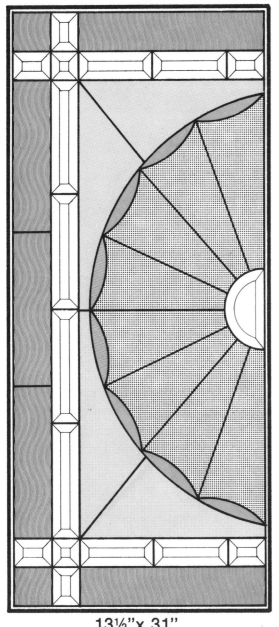
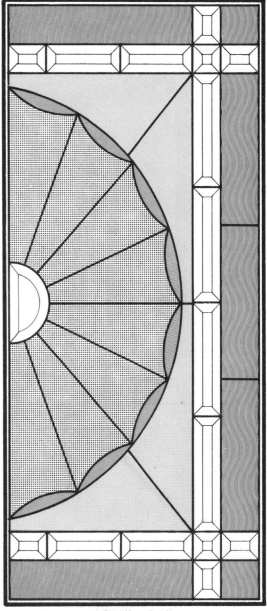

13½"x 31" 13½"x 31"

13"x 17"

13"x 17"

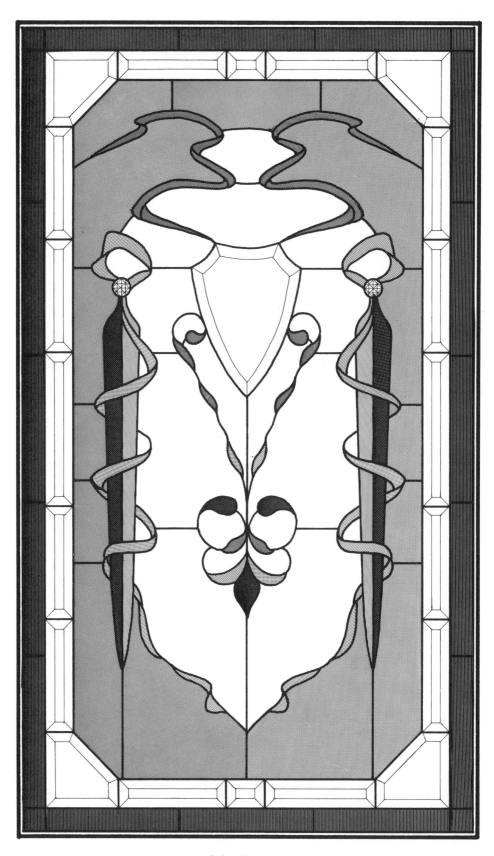

24½"x 42"

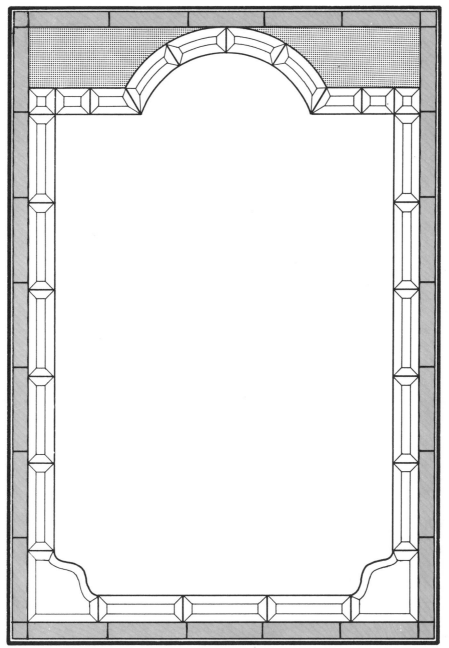

23"x 33"

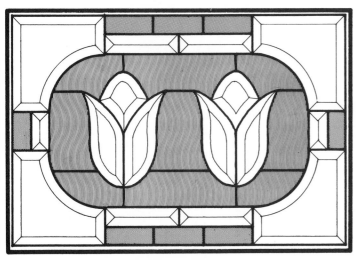

12"x 18"

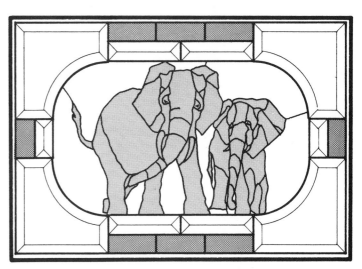

12"x 18"

23"x 33"

12"x 18"

12"x 18"

12"x 18"

23"x 33"

12"x 18"

10"x 40"

10"x 40"

27"x 27"

17½"x 20¼"

27"x 27"

17½"x 20¼"

15"x 42"

Center bevel clusters are two
#44's rearranged.

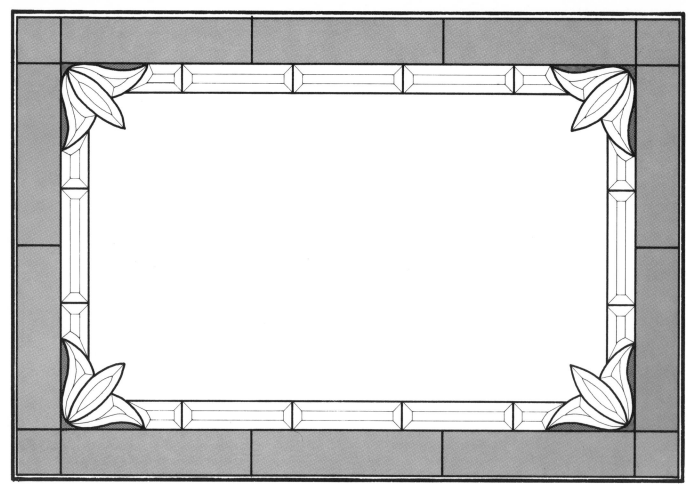

24"x 36"

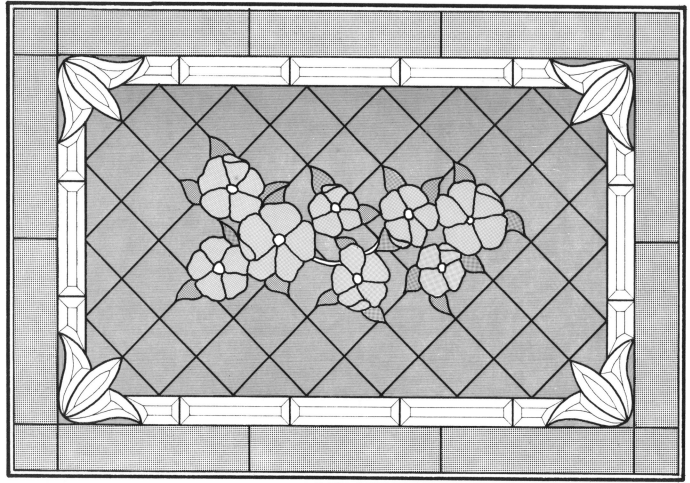

24"x 36"

24"x 36"

24"x 36"

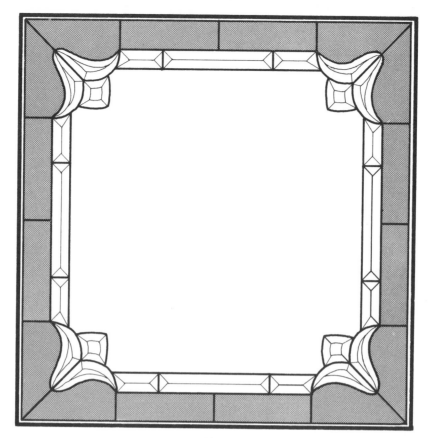

21"x 21"

21"x 21"

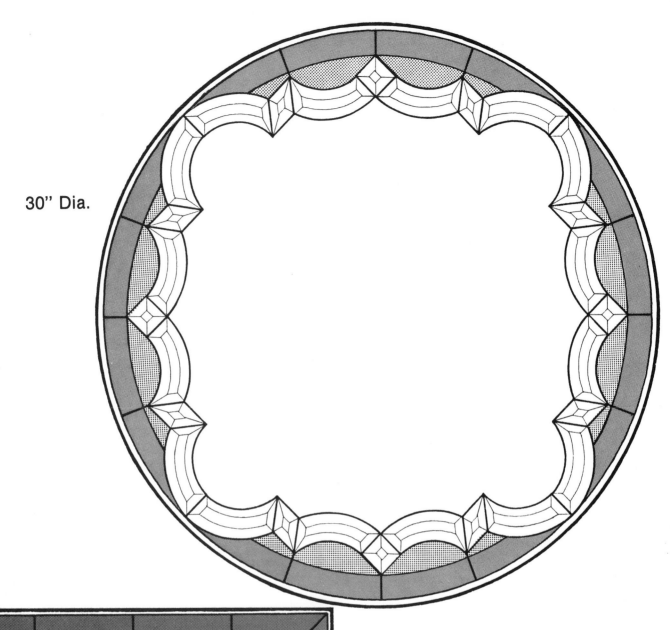

30" Dia.

21"x 21"

30" Dia.

21"x 21"

20"x 36¼"

20"x 36¼"

24"x 36"   Corners are bevel cluster #1

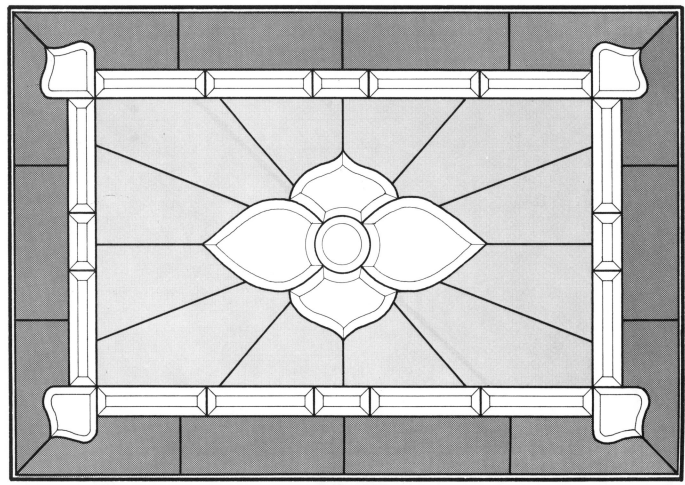

24"x 36"

34"x 34"

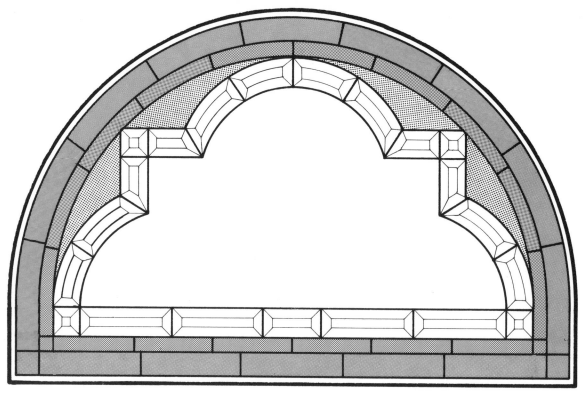

18¾"x 30"

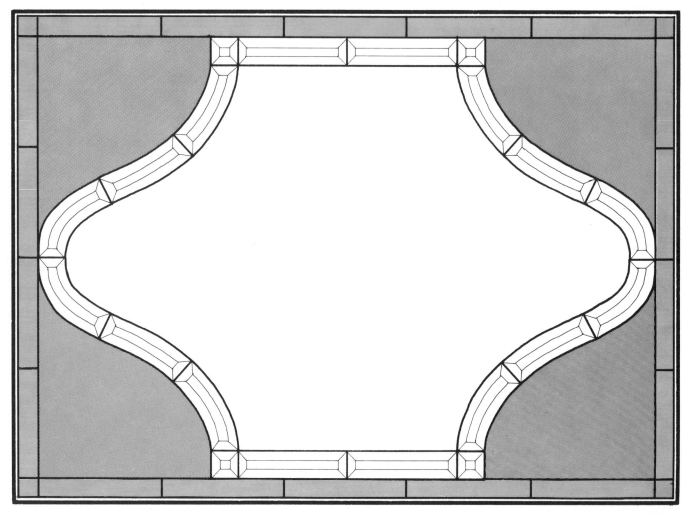

25"x 36"

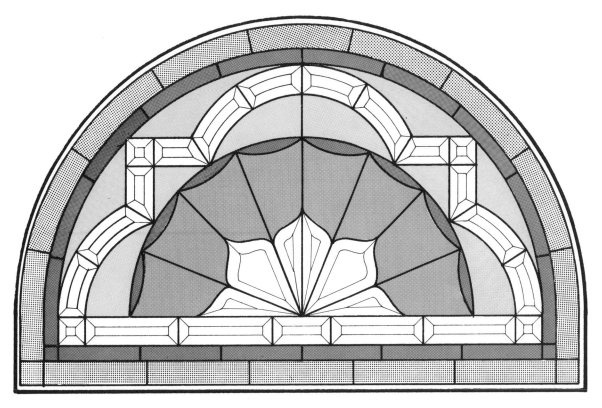

18¾"x 30"

25"x 36"

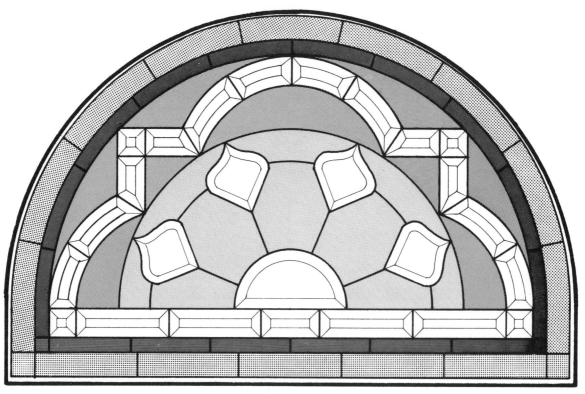

18¾"x 30"

25"x 36"

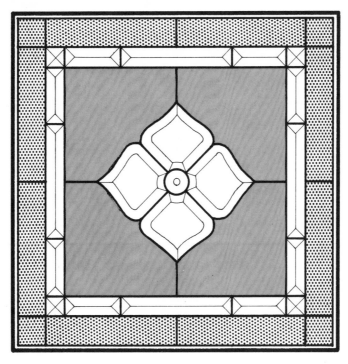

17"x 17"

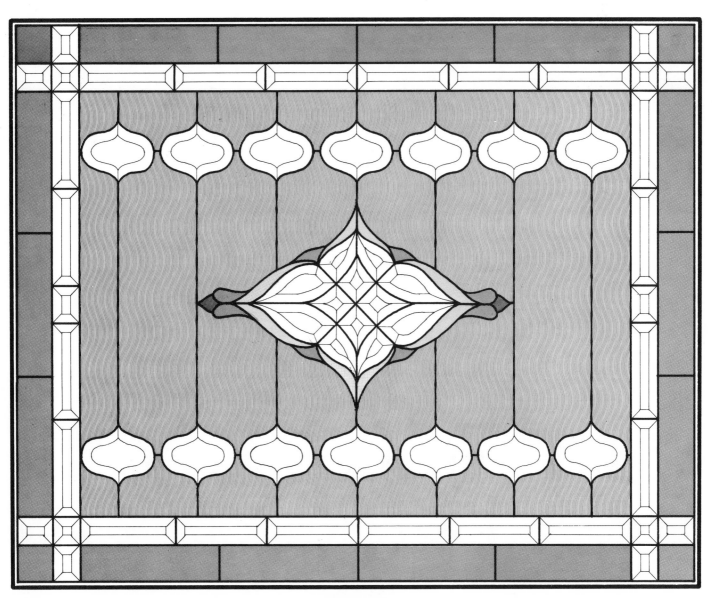

29"x 37"

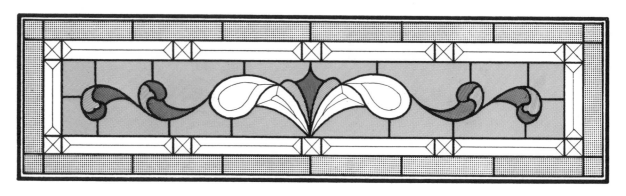

8"x 31"

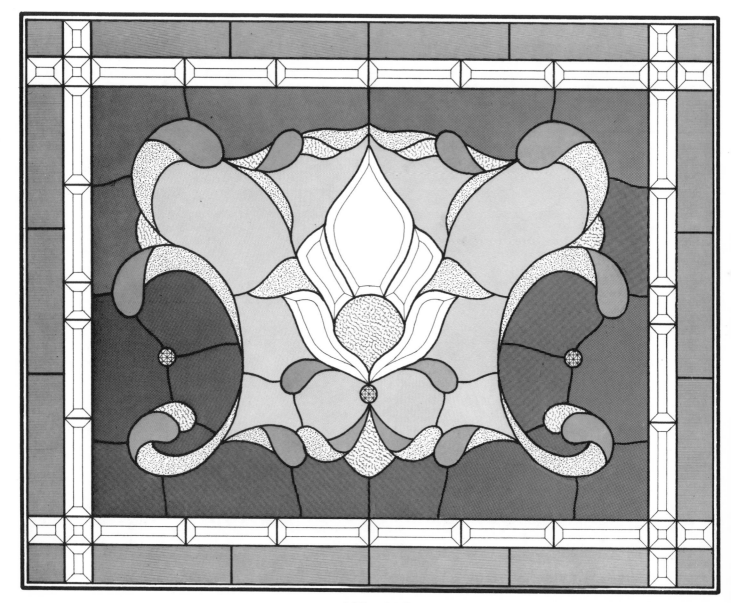

29"x 37"

8"x 31"

34"x 34"

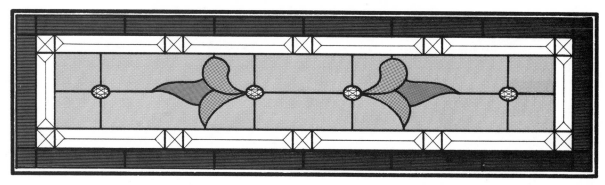

8"x 31"

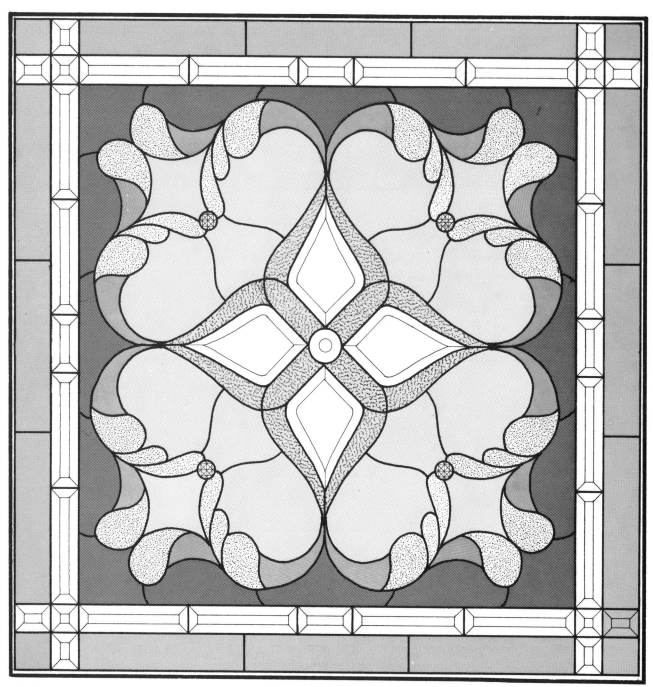

34"x 34"

CENTER CLUSTERS

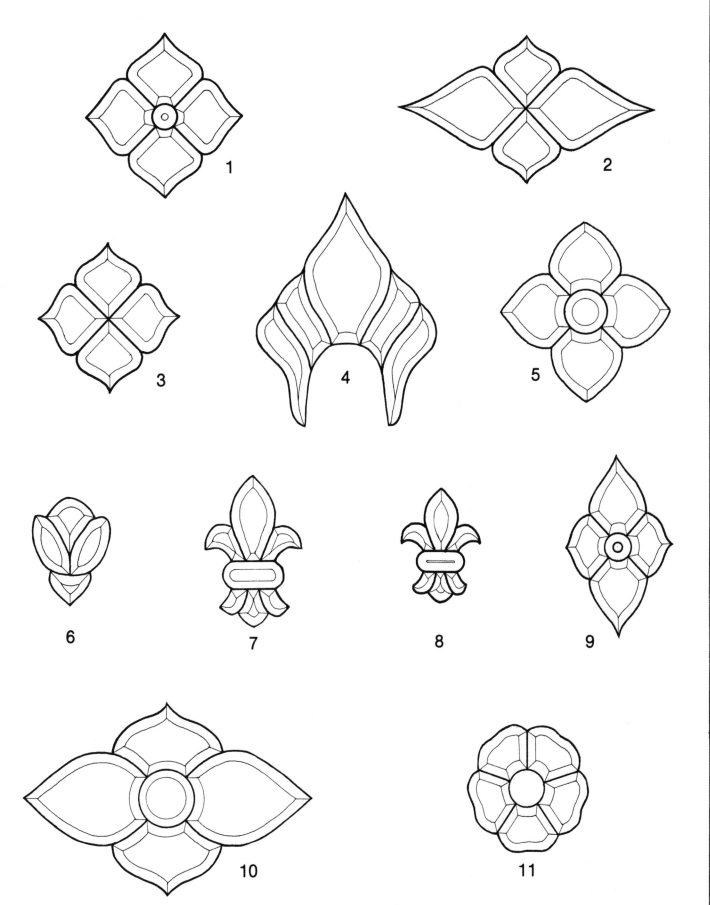

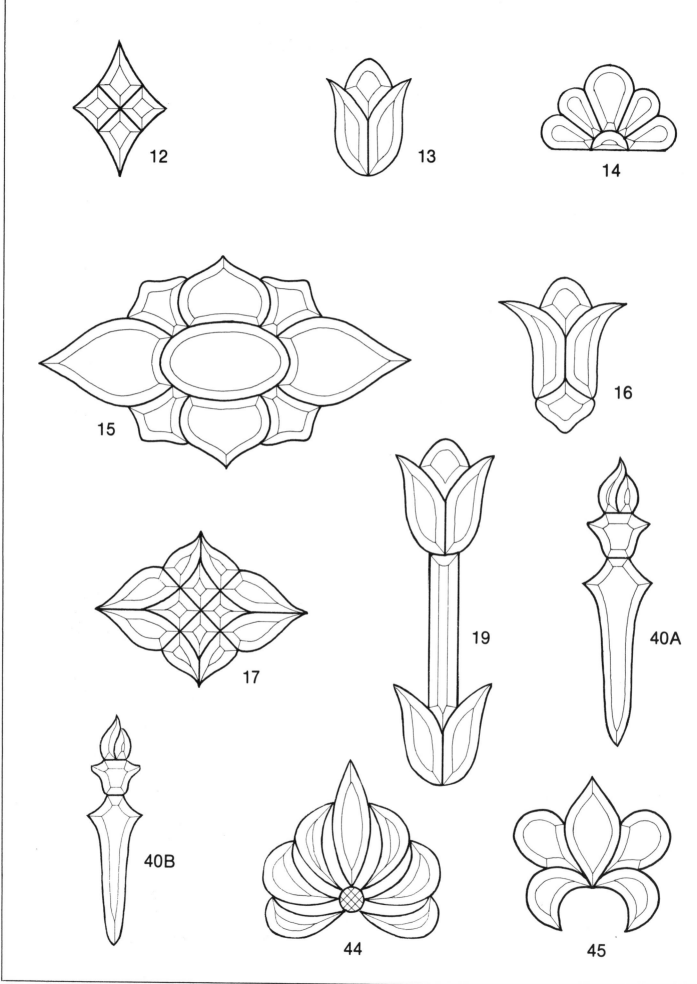

12

13

14

15

16

17

19

40A

40B

44

45

CORNERS

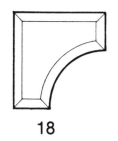 18

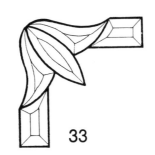 33

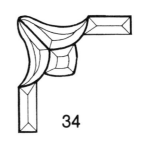 34

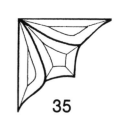 35

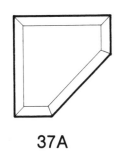 37A

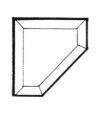 37B

 37C

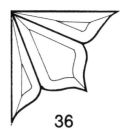 36

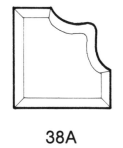 38A

 38B

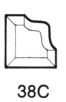 38C

 41A

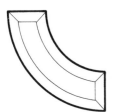 39A

 39B

 39C

 41B

ACCENT PIECES

42

43

46

47

CRESTS

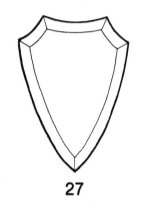

27

28A

28B

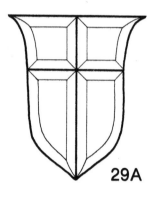

29A

29B

30

31

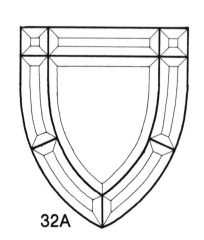

32A

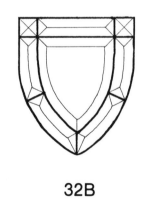

32B

FRAMES

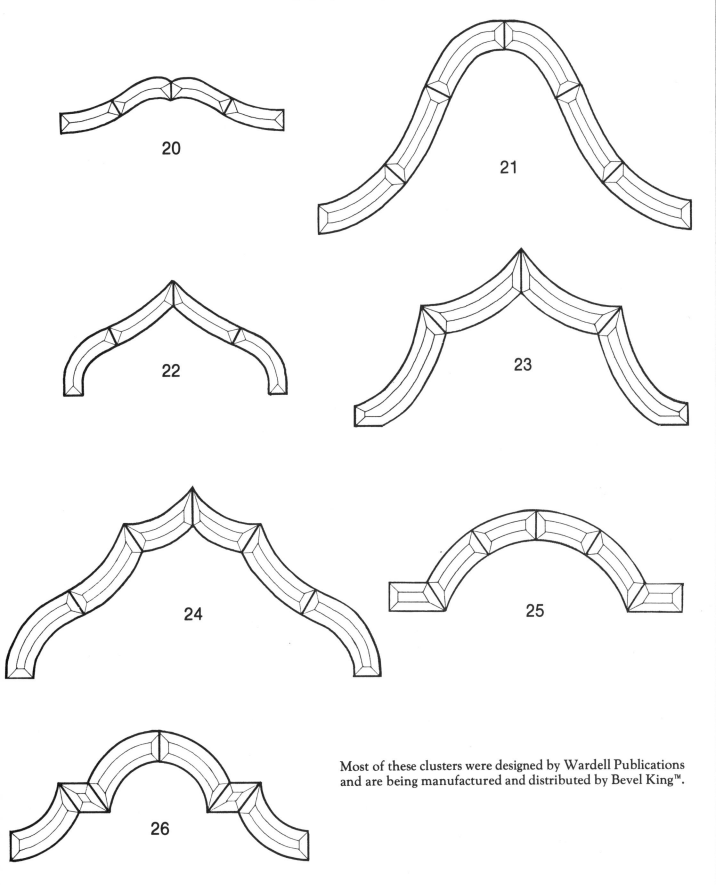

20

21

22

23

24

25

Most of these clusters were designed by Wardell Publications
and are being manufactured and distributed by Bevel King™.

26

STOCK BEVELS

DESCRIPTION	SIZE (Inches)		DESCRIPTION	SIZE (Inches)

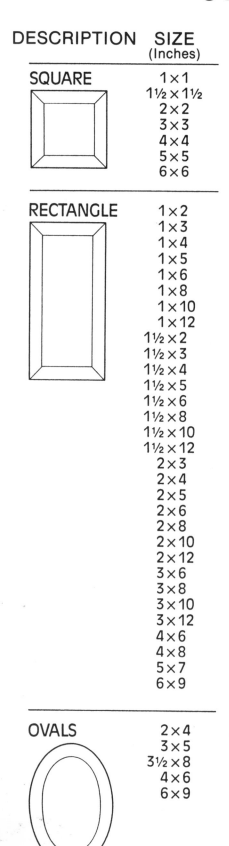

SQUARE
- 1 × 1
- 1½ × 1½
- 2 × 2
- 3 × 3
- 4 × 4
- 5 × 5
- 6 × 6

RECTANGLE
- 1 × 2
- 1 × 3
- 1 × 4
- 1 × 5
- 1 × 6
- 1 × 8
- 1 × 10
- 1 × 12
- 1½ × 2
- 1½ × 3
- 1½ × 4
- 1½ × 5
- 1½ × 6
- 1½ × 8
- 1½ × 10
- 1½ × 12
- 2 × 3
- 2 × 4
- 2 × 5
- 2 × 6
- 2 × 8
- 2 × 10
- 2 × 12
- 3 × 6
- 3 × 8
- 3 × 10
- 3 × 12
- 4 × 6
- 4 × 8
- 5 × 7
- 6 × 9

OVALS
- 2 × 4
- 3 × 5
- 3½ × 8
- 4 × 6
- 6 × 9

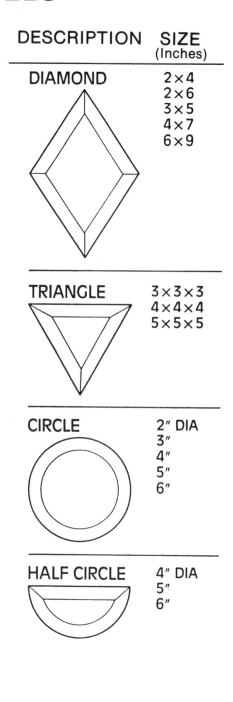

DIAMOND
- 2 × 4
- 2 × 6
- 3 × 5
- 4 × 7
- 6 × 9

TRIANGLE
- 3 × 3 × 3
- 4 × 4 × 4
- 5 × 5 × 5

CIRCLE
- 2" DIA
- 3"
- 4"
- 5"
- 6"

HALF CIRCLE
- 4" DIA
- 5"
- 6"